MW00991072

1

Tie Your Shoes Kid

Poems by Meta Sarmiento

ISBN 978-1-365-99282-7

Acknowledgements

I'm at a point in life where I truly believe I cannot accomplish much on my own, especially when it comes to creating. There's a handful of people who've helped me with putting this collection together, from its content to its final presentation. Without them, this wouldn't exist.

Thank you Mommy and Pa for doing what you could to give me a fighting chance at life. Thank you Kuya, Amanda, and baby Rosa for being a piece of home in a city so unfamiliar. Thank you Ate, Ponce, baby Grace, Noah, and Elijah for welcoming me into your new home and giving me the space to take this collection into finality. Thank you Tiffany for being so supportive in the few months I went broke and literally hungry trying to bring this all to life. Thank you Diego for being the first homie away from home. Thank you Aubrey for your loving friendship which strengthened me to keep walking in the moments I reached for my white flags.

They say it takes a village. You are my village. Thank you for being everything I needed to push new work into the sun. I hope it makes you laugh and cry and argue and contemplate and proud. I hope it makes you feel. Something. Anything. I love you. So much.

Leaving

I decided
to pack my entire life into one carry-on,
a check-in, and fit the rest of it in two *Balikbayan* boxes

and I wasn't headed to the Philippines
and I wasn't going for vacation
and the weight of not knowing what would survive the flight
was heavier than an island
rattling
through a plane's turbulent farewell.

And some days I feel like
drowning might be better than breathing.
Emptiness can take up so much room.

The hardest part about leaving isn't goodbye

it's saying hello
to a city
that does not welcome you home.

Where You From?

Is there such a thing as a cultural refugee?
To be born a twisted kaleidoscope,
pulled from a womb that was stretched
between too much history?

Sometimes I'm not sure if I can call any place home.
If no man is an island why can he be abandoned like one?
Why can he be invaded like one?
Why can he be torn apart and rebuilt into a base like one?

I tell people I'm trilingual, my tongue is a shape shifter,
Hello ang pangalan ko ay Meta sumasaga yu' giya Dededo.
What's good I'm from the North side of Guam,
from Mabini Street, from a village full of immigrants.

At dinner, we watch The Filipino Channel.
Nightly news is a lesson on heritage.
There are more homeless children in Manila
than there are students in every Guam public school combined.
There is a civil war in Southern Philippines
and the casualties aren't always soldiers.
Every Christmas, celebrities sing a new song
about the strength and love of the Filipinos,
how a prospering nation is one of Christ's greatest gifts.

At school I avoid the FOBs,
those kids that bring their accents with them.
Hate their perfume. Hate their loudness.
Hate they could go back to the Philippines
and not be treated like a tourist.

In Guam, tourism is a pillar of the economy.
The other pillar is militarization.
A tourist is just a temporary immigrant.
A permanent immigrant is a temporary native.
Guam enlists more natives into the United States Armed Forces
per capita than any place in America.
Are you from a military town? I'm from a military island.
Maybe you can relate when I say
we go to war for presidents we aren't allowed to vote for.
Maybe you can't.

I tell people I'm trilingual, my voice is a chameleon,
Hello I can speak jungle hotel room service and atomic bomb.
What's good I'm from the North side of Guam,
from mothers who cha cha with the poverty line
and fathers who still fish for hope,
from daughters who dance like the wind,
from sons who rise like morning.

I'm a small and skinny kid, could make spears from my shin bones
and sip coconut water from my sunken cheeks.
I wish someone told mom
giving birth to me meant raising a wild thing,
meant my place of origin would take too much explaining,
meant you'd have to fall in love with me
to understand where I'm from

because the only way to grasp all the violence in my history
is if you have enough compassion to accept the blood.
When they ask where I'm from, I say
from Guam and the Philippines.
I say I'm an Asian American Pacific Islander
and most days

that

is enough.

Watch Your Mouth

In my class, Jeremy never sits in the same seat.
It's like each desk is a house he can't afford so
he's always moving. I guess
he got used to moving growing up
because his mom
couldn't pay rent.

I ask myself
how could I make a class feel like home
if a kid doesn't know what home
is supposed to feel like in the first place?
He hates being here. Hates his work, his uniform,
he hates all his teachers. But he says *Sir!*
I like you sir. You're fuckin' badass!
I say *Jeremy!*

Watch

your

mouth.

He says
What channel?!

I say a*ny channel Jeremy, any, but please*
just not the news.

Jeremy totes a gang sign like a hand gun,
brushes grades off like dust in a street fight.
He thinks a snapback is more stylish than a grad cap.
He says *Sir! Fuck an A. I'm a G.*
And I get where Jeremy's coming from.
I've seen hard times and empty pockets turn heroes
into villains. Kids trade capes for rags
'til they learn to save themselves.
When I was a young buck
I helped my homie steal clothes from the mall
'cause his mom couldn't buy him any.

Money was tighter than our fists clenched in a riot,
budgets cut like our lips in a street fight. Blood
and failing are two things I'm very familiar with.
So when I see Jeremy passed out
sleeping on a desk, I get angry
'cause that's not what I meant when I said
you need to dream. So I tell him

Jeremy. Wake up. I know life's hard
but you can't crumple like paper.
You don't belong in a trash bin.
You're not someone else's garbage.
Don't recycle your OG's history.

I got respect for your gang's flag and I believe
in the promise of brotherhood, but brothers
should keep you safe
not dare you to rot in a prison cell. Wake up.

If you must steal, go steal a book from the library!
And why don't you break your back like a jaw
'til you can help your mom pay the bills.
Don't you know?

You could be a politician
or a doctor or a business man? But first
you gotta be a better man.
The world is so much bigger than the girls you fuck
and punks you knock out.
You'll miss the most amazing things in life
with your eyes shut so tightly. So unclench them.
Get up. Slowly but surely the same way the sun
yawns light into your small apartment.

And quit fighting so damn much.
You can't love the things you never hold.
So open your fists.

And Jeremy, I'm not saying put your hands down
I'm saying use them for a better purpose.
I mean c'mon! How the hell can you make it out there
if you can't even make it in here?!

I say all this to him with my hands in his face,
my finger pointed at him like a gun
and he goes *Sir! This is why you're fuckin badass!*

And I say *Jeremy!*

Watch

your

mouth.

Chores

I am eight
and before I could watch Saturday morning cartoons
I have to help sis clean the entire house.
Big bro is 18 and earned his right to sleep in,
but I'll bang the broomstick against his door
every time I sweep near his room.

I guess doing chores is a lesson on work ethic
and commitment. Mom says even if a house is poor,
clean it like a palace. Wipe the wood
like it's gold. Nothing here shines on its own,
only the moon, only the change in the piggy bank,
everything else takes work.

So I clean, put on the music, play Lauryn Hill
and Doo-wop dirt into the dustpan,
scrub the toilet, take the trash out, tell the homies
I'll be back before sunset.

I am eight and before permission
I say please and after it's given I say thank you.
I tell mom ten years from now
I won't be sleeping in on Saturdays. I don't know yet
that I am dead wrong.

I sit at the table, have *Doug* and *Recess* for breakfast
when my sis smacks my head, pats it after and says *You dummy.*
You missed a spot.

Tie Your Shoes Kid

I fall with my mouth open. I taste the rocks and grass and choke
on their laughter. School aides ask what happened
and none of the kids admit to punching me in the back of my head.
They say nothing, that I just tripped on my laces.

I'm so nervous I forget to kick my Vans off.
We fall into each other's mouths and I think rough and loud
and give her what the porn vids taught me,
but her body softens like
it finally made it back to shore after being lost at sea
and I learn that not every girl wants to be owned.
She presses her thumb to my chin, wants to know
if I heard the stories about her ex boyfriend,
if I can fill the shoes he left behind
with something more than angry hands.

I press tissues against Romel's bloody forehead.
His mouth opens, pleads not to call the ambulance,
says his dad would kill him like
we didn't just try to beat him to death.
The whole crew howls like a pack of wolves
'cause now we know he's down for the block.
Give enough blood to a stranger and he'll call you brother.
Take enough kicks to the ribs and see
if loyalty rattles like a rusty cage.
I don't see Romel anymore, not ever, not anywhere.

I raise a bottle in the air like a trophy
and Pa says he's proud of me,
looks at me like
he can't believe I made it through high school,
like stories about sons who get lost and never come home
are about me
like dear God thank you
for letting that bullet hit someone else.
I wear my church shoes to graduation. The ceremony
feels like an answer to all of mom's praying.

    I let my mouth catch water that locals say is blessed by mountains.
    Dr. Johnson says even if I'm not religious, I can pray,
    that prayer is not knocking on Heaven's door with a plea bargain.
    Prayer is the practice of forgiving yourself.
    This trip to Bali is part university research
    and part reflection. I ask my eyes not to break like mirrors.
    They don't listen and the memories are shards.
    They carve regrets into my cheekbones.
    I drown the temple's prayer pools in apologies.
    I say forgive me for hurting Christine and every woman after,
    for almost killing someone who might have been a friend,
    for making Mom and Pa question God's intentions. I say
    forgive me for promising my heart but lending my body,
    for always saying sorry and never meaning the word,
    for claiming to be a great man but failing so much
    at proving it. I say if I ever come back to visit
    my list will be short and my eyes will be quiet.
    The footsteps I take into prayer will be steady
    like the base
    of a blessed mountain.

Mom and the Quiet Mass

Mom finally accepted my absence at the pews,
knows that I only ever attend mass
when someone's graduating, getting married, or dead.

I know it was hard for her,
how heavy her hand was when she slapped me,
brought the weight of pure devotion
down against my cheekbone.
I didn't say a word, let the sting on my skin
linger, let the quiet tears fill the distance stretched between us.
Maybe I should have said I'm sorry, should have said
I promise
refusing church doesn't mean
quitting my search for peace or abandoning my commitment
to loving others like heaven was already in me.

Today she asks
does my dress match my heels?

I say
you're too pretty even for angels.

I say
you might make the priest a sinner again!

And I tell her to bring an umbrella
and her laughter rings out
like homilies reviving faith in nonbelievers

and she says *No no no*

the rain
is God's blessing.

Papa and the First Flight

The first time Pa got on a plane
he was leaving the country that raised him.

In *Tagalog*, there is no word for
goodbye

Only *Paalam*

And *Makita tayo ulit*

Only *I'm leaving*

And *Let's see each other again.*

Mamay and the Quick Knife

Grandma chased Pa with a machete up a tree once.
That stern old woman
knew to drive a blade through a man's chest
before she learned to cut hearts from paper,
knew to question all faith except the one in God
'cause too many men were drunks and liars,
even the priests, but never the church.
The holy spirit always walked a straight line.
The prayers were always sober.

That hard old Pinay who
after wrinkles put wisdom in her
quit on hate
like Gramps did his bottle.

She started asking Pa
to help pick fruit from the backyard's afternoon.

And even with the mountain
growing in her back
we knew
she could always reach
the sun.

Kuya and the Snowy Mountain

When I was 15, my parents sent me to Japan
to spend my first winter with my big bro,
the Jet Fighter Technician stationed in Misawa.

It was the first time I heard him tell his friends
I was his baby brother, first time he opened a beer for me
and asked what I wanted to be when I grew up.
I said *I don't want to be a shadow. I don't want to be a comparison.*
I said *I want to be a writer like you but most like myself.*

And we travelled through the country side in a beat up Jeep,
by snow walls as high as houses, along rivers that slowed like
 a sleeping heart. And he took me to a ramen house
where the owners made their own noodles, never asked for my ID,
and he told me the weather has no feelings,
how working inside a jet intake in zero degrees
makes you miss the island, how yearning for warmth long enough
teaches you to build your own fire.

And the Hachimantai Forest swallowed me like a cave.
After falling hundreds of times the snowboard on my feet
finally felt like something I could control. And I coasted
through the snow with the sky watching, with the wind
pushing at my back.

And it's still the most beautiful winter I ever experienced,
strapped in below the peak, the island boy
sitting so high above sea level,
hearing my brother ask
are we moving through the mountain
or is the mountain moving through us?

Under Midnight

My big sis pointed at the midnight above us
and shouted *make a wish! Shooting star!*
I don't remember what I wished for.
Maybe a bike Mom couldn't afford
or a new toy before Christmas
or a real drum set for my birthday,

but I remember asking how something so far away
could make my wish come true. Since then

I've wondered why we throw our wishes
at something so temporary;
why we look at stars like open hands
and think anything could survive in the fire.

Maybe we feel drawn to them
because we know it's a miracle
for light to dance so brightly
in such intense darkness.
Maybe they remind us
of ourselves,
just flashing neon signs that say

you've been here before,
paralyzed in an emptiness that had no end,
stuck and suffocating in darkness
with no way out

and yet you survived,
lit your white flag til the quit in you burned
into dust and then into nothingness

Maybe
you're so obsessed with the magic in the sky
because up
is the only direction you ever wish to go.

You search and search until you realize
all the glimmering is just a mirror
and you finally see yourself in all the shine,
how maybe
you're destined to fade too,
but before you disappear,
you're meant to be a mark of hope
for the rest of history to reflect on.

Maybe that's it.

Maybe that's why you're so drawn to the sky;
so quick to throw a wish to a faraway flame

because

it mimics *you*

And maybe

you're the miracle

that taught the stars

how to fall.

You Deserve Tomorrow

I know you think there's nothing after this,
that the light at the end of the tunnel is useless 'cause the walls
are collapsing. You've given yourself to others so many times
and now you just want to be selfish. You don't want to be hurt
ever again and I know because I've been there before.

I've sliced my skin and have watched blood sing across the tiles.
I've felt my pulse hang and quiet like the last song.
Problems have such a loud voice and right now
all you want is silence. You feel betrayed
by a love you thought was loyal,
broken and abandoned like an old promise
and how can you be willing to go on?

How do you breathe with shattered glass in your lungs?
How do you smile with a rusty cage inside your throat?
It's hard to stand straight when even daylight feels heavy.
When the sadness finds your bones the tremble in your knees
makes it hard to walk and you're tired of trying

so tired of pretending that you have it all together,
that you're still here, that you're still you,
that you're not the shattered mirror
or the box cutter,
that you're just fine, still healing,
still refusing the echo of an empty pill bottle

that you haven't been speeding past power poles wondering
at what speed is death a guarantee?
And I know because I've been there before:

at the edge of the cliff asking the moon
how many bodies shatter against the ocean's caress?
Falling is so much easier than flying, but don't do it.

Just close your eyes.
Remember who you'll become after this moment.
This isn't the first coffin in your chest you've had to survive.
Your heart is more than a graveyard.
There is still life in your smile.
Don't let your dreams go out like funeral candles.

You deserve tomorrow.

Don't ever forget that.

You deserve tomorrow,

to catch the moon in your palms
ask it how much laughter has the sky embraced lately?
How lonely has the cliff become
now that you're back from the edge?

There is value in your breath.
There is so much more to your story than heartache and surrender.
You have so much more to look forward to:

the success, the triumphs, the happiness

the tremble in your bones from dancing midnight into dawn

the wrinkles near your eyes, lifelines carved by wisdom.

Remember who you'll become after this moment.

Remember

you

deserve

tomorrow.

A Bad Influence on My Nephew

Dear Eli,

I know how heavy it gets, being so small
and you'll feel that weight one day
when he breaks your nose and tells the principal you fell,
when everybody watches, but nobody helps.

And I wish others would stop believing
violence is the only proof of strength,
but the world we live in is not always so kind.
I'd rather you be prepared than broken.

That's why I'm teaching you how to throw a punch now
because for small kids like us,
poetry will never stop a fist
or a bat
or a bullet.

My notebook never kept bad intentions
from tearing through my body
so before you're old enough to aim a gun,
I'll teach you how to make hammers out of your fists.
And when people tell you to be the bigger man,
you remind them how much blood the bigger men took from you.

But for now
don't be sorry for the size of your bones.
Save your apologies for real mistakes.
You're not God's accident.
Your hands are more than white flags.
Your voice is more than a helpless plea.
Don't let anyone tell you that you are too small to be powerful.
Remember, your blood is my blood

and our blood is a history of overcoming conquests.
So when giants think to ruin you like a village,
you call on the fight in your veins.

You bear your knuckles like teeth.
You defend that valley in your heart.
You teach them being big
has nothing to do with how close we stand to the sky.

But remember there's more to fighting
than bruises or blood,
more to defend than pride and body.
Strength goes deeper than what your hands can split.

Remind them
strength
is more than muscle breaking bone,
more than the glory of destruction.
Remind them
strength
is love too,
the capacity to accept others for who they are,
the ability to create meaning
out of thin air.

Remind them
strength
means being a good eldest brother,
teaching family how to make music
from all the world's silence.

You shed those tears, Elijah,
but you give them back to the ocean

And don't you ever forget

the depth of your fighting spirit
cannot be caged in the measurements of man.

If Ever I Have a Daughter

I'll tell her
Girl! What the fuck are you wearing?!
It's nice! Be proud of what momma gave you.
Let 'em all know where you get it from!
Show 'em all that in our house
we measure dignity with the integrity of our character
not by the inch of a skirt!
Let 'em all know

Your body
belongs to you.
Values are deeper than skin
and when we talk self-respect
we ask if our bones are fit for building temples.
You know the difference between worship and thirsty prayer.
Tell 'em you are not a goddess.
You are a warrior the goddess fears.

Tell that boy he is not a key. You are not a lock.
You are a vault
and the only combination to open you up
starts and ends with consent.

Sometimes being comfortable in your skin
means people will feel uncomfortable in theirs.
They will turn the self-hate outward and call it advice,
call it everything except a shallow reflection.
This is not your fault.
People rarely accept
what they wish they could be.

They don't think your brown is gold enough
but will try to mine diamonds from all your sand.
Your skin says there's some island inside you.
We know what invaders make of paradise;
Make it their own, plant seeds, call the invasion a gift.

Remember, the sweet center of a coconut
only comes after the husking. There is nothing easy about you.
Men will see the challenge as invitation,
will praise your flesh so long as you remain the exotic fantasy

But you are more than postcard dinner show.
You are raging ocean
and you are allowed to demand respect
like a storm at sea.

You are allowed to put your heart and your mind
before anyone else's.
Just promise me that when I'm old and gray
you save some space for me, somewhere.
Keep me in a picture frame, in a wallet,
in a journal entry, in a dream.
Promise you'll try to visit me
and you'll say

Pops. I met this man and he respects me
and the only thing he's ever forced onto me
is bad music and burnt cooking
and he reminds me of how you treat mom
and he says that when we have a daughter,
he'll read that one poem you never finished writing, the one for me,
the one about that horrible skirt you let me wear to the mall.
Do you remember?

Do you remember?

When She Asks Where We Come From

I'll blow against the rim of an emptying wine bottle,
tell her it's the sound the wind makes
at the edge of the harbor's mouth.

I'll take her to the cemetery,
show her where the flowers go,
how the space between a finger
and a petal
is enough room to measure the distance
between what we remember
and what we have yet to figure out.

When He Asks Where We Come From

I'll cup my hand around his ear
and tell him to listen.

I'll show him the sharpest rock in the backyard,
how its rough edges feel the same
as coral
from the ocean's open chest

and I'll ask him to hold his breath
to fill his lungs
like a harbor
at high tide.

This Place, This Beach

This strip of a million years,
of dead things from the sea,
this stretch of rolling history,
this source of game-board hour glass,

where kids build castles out of sand
and become the royalty that existed
before the soldiers and sickness came,

this harbor for a broken heart,
this place of celebration,
this deep blue Sunday where I first learned
what it meant to keep my head above water,
this crystal clear memory

is home

even after trading salt for the city

it's still home

even after the house is built farthest

from shore.

Guahan

We may have planted our seeds
but we do not own the soil.
We may have learned the language
but we do not own the mouths
that birthed it.

And if we believe in this island's spirit,
in the depth of the word home,
then we should learn to step aside
and let the navigators
choose
what wind
fills the sail next.

Myself and the Raging Temper

Maybe lineage means being a shadow
of someone we never really knew.
Grandpa was a photo album
and vacations to the Philippines.

I hear I inherited his bad temper,
that mom was too busy to breast feed me
and if she had
maybe I wouldn't be so thirsty for a fight.

In a town too poor for therapy
drinking on the couch
was the cheapest form of coping.

When you mix a bad temper with alcohol
you get a lonely ballad of bruises.
Men in my family talk with their fists much too often
and the women can sing the sea silent.
I never imagined I could force my lover
to cry the same song.

The first time she was terrified of me,
I had one hand locked around her wrist
and one hand gripping her throat.
The thunder in my breath
shook the ocean from her eyes
and in that moment
I was an echo of my Grandpa's rage,
a branch of the family tree
where Love stopped growing.

Maybe lineage is history repeating itself.
Maybe lineage is inheriting bones built for breaking.
Maybe I was always meant to swing,
to calm angry fists by steeping them in whiskey.

She asked me what I was doing.
She asked me if this is how it would always be,
if I could ever change,
if I could be better than the stories of drunk and angry men.

And my only response was crying beneath the weight of guilt,
was asking myself how to get rid of the hands passed down to me,
asking if lineage
was just another excuse
to forgive my bad decisions,
yet another scapegoat to acquit
my lack of control.

I plead for her to stay, tell her I can be better,
that my search for exits in empty bottles
ends here,
that the song she sings next
will not be choked
from her tightening throat.

She says maybe one day she'll believe me, but not tonight,
not with the anger in my voice, not with the marks I left on her skin.
She says goodbye forever
and maybe
this is what lineage really is

taking the blame for the trauma
and begging for forgiveness.

Enduring Storms

I almost died in a typhoon once. I was only 7 years old.
We lived on the second story of our building,
couldn't afford storm shutters,
so we used plywood to cover our windows and doors.
But the winds pried at our protection, ripped at our safety
and turned it into a question of survival. I answered by
grabbing a hammer and nails and ran outside with my father.

The trees and power poles bowed,
guilty subjects in front of their queen.
The rain, an army of arrows,
pinned me to the edge of our floor
and dared my father to come save me from falling.
I still remember the quake in his grip as he reached me just in time.
I'm certain now that fear is colder than a raging storm.

Super typhoon *Paka* hit Guam in December 1997
and it was the darkest Christmas I ever experienced.
My island was torn open like a gift
and we struggled to find smiles in all of its shreds.
Storms in the Pacific have increased in both frequency and strength.
Super typhoon *Soudelor*, *Vongfong*, *Yolanda*; track each storm,
each point a pendant, devastation strewn like a necklace
across our map. Regions are choking on gust and gale.

The carnage you see from behind the safety of your screen
is born in our ocean. Rising temperatures are heating our waters
and a warmer ocean is open invitation for more punishing rain.

A storm is the tragic love story between sea and sky,
a reminder that we cannot master nature.

We can only endure it.

An Ode to NCS, Dededo

When Manny Pacquiao steps in the ring
he fights for God, country, and Dededo!
Here's to my Northside Flips,

for the mothers who wake up early
to save a spot at the laundromat,
for the naked babies running in the weekend rain,
for the gritty clash between cement and jungle,
for kids who want everything and parents
who can't afford much.

I learned to fight here, ate my first punch
behind my bestfriend's house,
had my first kiss on Finegayan's playground,
learned to chase a thief
and beat out a sorry from his crying mouth.

For the street before all the new housing,
before land owners figured to build cheap,
charge high, and offer to military families.

For when the 7-11 store was our bus stop,
when breakfast was an arcade game
and we spent our lunch money
playing Street Fighter II before school.

For Mabini Street. For Rizal Street. For Quezon Street.
For the signs along the road
that said
this is the beginning of the heartaches
that legends are made of.

Brace yourself kid. The world
is big and loud and it's ready to grind that smile
into dust.

150 Miles per Hour

Winds are most dangerous at the wall of the eye
but even so
when it finally passes over the island
we go outside to see what the first half of the typhoon
decides to leave us.

A dead dog against a twisted tin roof,
a windshield swallowing a power pole,
an empty house with a ceiling collapsed on family photos.

We hope the schools that serve as shelters
for the families who can't afford safety hold up.
We know how old the schools are,
how even those buildings can cave under enough pressure.

And when the winds begin to howl again
like a hungry beast
we scurry back inside and brace for what the storm takes next.

The doors cannot keep the water out.
We wring the towels until our hands are close to bleeding,
until our muscles know the threat of flood.
We work and eat in shifts, keep the lighters and candles in bags,
keep the board games and cards in the top cabinets,
keep as much meat as we can on ice
and save the canned goods for last.
We know the most punishing point of a storm
is living through the damage.

When the radio broadcasts return,
we scan the waves for news of a body count
and pray that the help our neighbors need
when it's all over
will not involve coffins.

In the Sand

I picture you with water around your ankles,
kids throwing seaweed and *balate'* at each other,
cousins strumming guitars and singing out of tune.

The sky is pink and purple and the smoke from the grill
is the color of clouds before the downpour.
You are drifting between this beach
and the bedroom we hid in during the tropical depression.
Your grandma is yelling for you to put clothes on,
but your skin is drinking the sunset now
and the swirl of sand and music is more important
than her old biases. Your body is beautiful,
the scars, curves, stretch marks,
the tingle my lips left on places you didn't think
they could ever crave.

Your uncles yell *Hoy! Come and eat!*
And all the kids flock like wild chickens.
Your feet leave prints between the water's lapping
and the edge of the party table. Your grandma says grace,
asks God to protect the food and family and you whisper
the beach too.

I picture you with a mouth full of red rice and barbecue
and choking back laughter 'cause your nephew
falls backwards in his chair and cries mostly over his spilled food.
You don't want to leave because these moments
keep you tethered to hoping. If God had to rest on the seventh day
he might have slept here, by the sea
and even if religion can't move you like the sky can
you swear there's something holy here, something in the wind
that says peace
is your set of worries stripped, naked
just like the sand.

Before the Whistle

I imagine the flags on the moon
disintegrating now into something like dust,

not quite pixie
or magic
or star.

More bits of limestone
like the powder that school aides
used to sift onto their betel nut
right before they'd blow their whistles
and scream *stop jumping off the swings*!

Us, flying up into the sky
like astronauts,

like we hadn't learned quite yet
how to fear heights or how to be so afraid

of gravity.

Friendship

Do you remember when
we were all we had?
Before the careers and pressures of marriage,
before airport terminals and goodbyes?

It's like somebody hit fast forward
and I can't remember when the scripts all changed.
We watch each other now from a distance
like neighbors who can't remember names.
I mow the lawn and wonder why we drowned our nights
with promises of forever so quickly,
with no hesitation, with no second guessing,
held troubles by the bottle neck
and toasted smiles at the sky.

It might have been naive to think
that we could always be there for each other,
that you would always come for me when I called.

But we're as close as the space between coasts now.
How can we grow together if we're so far apart?
We drifted, didn't we
like pieces of abandoned ships?
And none of us saw the rocks ahead,
just held onto old hope like a wheel before the crash.

I smile though, whenever I see young people
searching for the lighthouse in a friend.
I pray they find it and can say
time
is a test
they did not eventually fail.

The Lessons in Departures

Accept your own apologies.
Love ends with forgiveness.
Sometimes, home is a body and a voice.
Photographs are proof I am conquering my insecurities.
Going to bed after laughing helps me sleep better.
My insomnia is jealous of my dreams.
My passion has taken me farther than my fears ever have.
The only direction I wish to travel is forward, always.
Loneliness is an honest mirror.
They'll demand your love. You are not obligated to give it.
An expensive drink is still just cheap therapy.
The size of a house does not dictate how much happiness it can hold.
A healthy bird must leave its mother's nest.
Time is not the enemy. My lack of patience is.
Someone else's success is not my failure.
My heart deserves to smile after all it has survived.

A Letter to my Puppies

I'm writing to you 'cause I've been writing hella intense shit
for the last few weeks and my heart
is tired of visiting lonely places.

Here's a little celebration for
every time you pissed near my shoes and said
Yo take me on a freakin walk or at least rub my belly!
I'd be a liar if I said I didn't love you.

You're probably the only thing with a heartbeat
that still wants me even after all my yelling.
You tilt your head when I complain about life like
Dude quit being a punk ass and forget about it!

I mean, I know you only really love me
'cause I put food in your bowl, but I can tell
you hear the honesty in my laughter,
the pain in my good morning. You feel the shudder in my bones
when we sit by the window
and wait for people who aren't coming back.

I think that's why I keep you so close.
You lick my face and never ask if I'm okay
when clearly I'm not.
I know you're more affection than cloudy judgment.
And sometimes I need that more than people
'cause people are such unfair jurors.

So thanks. Thanks for being cute and loud and annoying.
I promise even after you've eaten through all my shoes,
you'll always have a space at the foot of my bed,
awake or asleep.
Always.

An Honest Job Interview

Tell me a little about yourself.

I'm from an invisible island. It's probably why my voice
demands so much to be seen. I grew up a five-minute walk
from a Navy communications base. At school, during recess
I'd run in the shadows of bombers flying toward the Airforce Base.
In high school, military recruiters promised that swearing in
meant college tuition was paid for. I never believed them.
My brother did and he didn't have the time to finish college
'cause he was busy fixing jets that bombed the Middle East.
If you press your ear against my chest, you can still hear the echo
of a ballet studio mom didn't want me joining. At the age of six,
Pa taught me my fists were large enough to keep love safe.
Use them for love, not on love sis would say.

What makes you a good candidate for this position?

I come from a line of fishermen and farmers. My hands
don't shy from hard work. There's no separating sacrifice
from passion. When I think of commitment, I see my parents
saying goodbye to the only home they ever knew.
I see them twisting their mouths around a language
that demands they forget a piece of themselves.
You want someone who knows where he comes from
and where he's headed. My ability to hold the past
in the present allows me a deeper perspective.
And don't you want that? Someone with eyes
that can see through yesterday?

How would other people describe you?

Pisces. Straight up. Small talk makes me uncomfortable.
I'm loving but seldom love people.
I'm friendly but rarely call people friends.
I've seemed happier lately, more optimistic about my chances.
I play nice with other kids. Maybe I dream too much,
let obsessions guide me more than facts.
I work too hard. I need more breaks.
I need to spend more time at parties and clubs and get a Snapchat.

What's your biggest accomplishment to date?

Standing in front of the mirror and not hating my reflection.
Stopped pretending my heart is on my sleeve,
rolled it up instead and got comfortable with bearing my scars
for those who won't abuse my weaknesses.
Forgiving myself for my bad decisions.
That's pretty huge no?
Admitting you made way too many mistakes
and finally escaping the prisons
you locked yourself in because of them.

Where do you see yourself in 5 years?

Alive? Smiling? Hopefully in love.
To be honest, I'm not quite sure.
I'm just trying to get through this month
one day at a time.

Across the Ocean

My heart broke from five thousand miles away
and the distance didn't quiet the pain

didn't stop me from shattering
like a bottle taking a bullet,
didn't stop me from collapsing like a roof
after too much rain.

But Pa wrote mom a thousand letters
when they were separated by an ocean

and hopefully one day
I'll find someone who'll stay
like the cursive goodbye
in old envelopes.

No Marble Statue

When you're both ready,
lay completely naked, face each other,
and don't speak a single word.

Love will not always look like this moment.
It will age. It will mature. It will wrinkle
and if you're only willing to sleep with a marble statue,
then get up, put your clothes on,
leave,
and never come back.

You both deserve happiness
that can smile through decay.

Fuse

Don't be fooled by the taste in his kiss.
It is not genius. It is not empathy.
It's only the dust that lingers from abandoned promises.

Maybe
he's just dynamite
and destroying what he loves
is the only way he knows how
to build something new.

Don't let him mine the soul from your heart.

You will not sleep soundly
after his flames turn your temple

into ruins.

He will light hope inside of you
and run

like it was a burning fuse.

Have You Apologized?

All your life,
you've never been one to give a second chance
And yet here you are, begging for one
hoping that cheating
can be forgiven.

You can't even pardon yourself of your crime
and you expect someone else to.
It's funny that you did exactly
what you promised you wouldn't do.

You deserted love for an escapade,
refused responsibility for a wild adventure.
Temptation is midnight dressed in red wine
and you couldn't refuse.
You poured your own half empty glass
and let one night with a stranger
drown a year with the woman who loved you most.

It wasn't their fault.
It was yours. You failed yourself.

You liar. You cheat. You worthless piece of shit.
Have you apologized yet?
Does the guilt have you believing in God again?
Are you praying for a way to travel back in time?
Do you realize that you're the source of trauma now?
You are the lie that emptied someone's faith.
Did you forget the weight of forever
when you got lost in a body that would leave at dawn?
Don't complain about the grave you dug for yourself.
You chose the shovel. You chose the coffin.
And I could only hope that after you suffocate enough
you excavate a version of yourself
that is better
than this skeleton.

Adrift

Momma said
be an ocean.

Step inside me and forget which way is up.
Close your eyes and drift
'til there's nothing but sky and waiting.

Know how that feels?

To come up for air and not know how far your breath took you?
To be surrounded by space so open
you forget which direction home is?

That might be what real love feels like

like being lost at sea,
both stranded and still utterly free.

Sing Me to Sleep

Returning to the right melody has saved me more than once
so I search for songs in everyone I meet,
open them up like the back of a dusty piano,

but I hear making a person your favorite song
is dangerous. What happens
when the record stops spinning?
When the music in the laughter
becomes faint and distant?

Yet here I am in love with your voice.
Your hello shifts my mood
like a moon tugging the tides.

I promise when we talk
I don't get sleepy because you bore me.
There's just a certain note your voice box plays
that gets me calm enough
to dream.

Rise

I imagine

when we finally make it

we'll fall to our knees

to remember all the lows

we fought so hard

to rise from.

A [Failed] Autobiography

I was born on the same day as Dr. Seuss. *Green Eggs and Ham* was my first real taste of poetry. I grew up in the village of Dededo, Guam. In every single grade level, I met teachers who convinced me I was too small to do anything different, that a Guam kid's future was either hotel management or the military. In 2007, as a high school Junior, I fell in love with poetry and decided I'd prove all those teachers wrong. I got my diploma from John F Kennedy High in 2008. I went on to receive a Bachelor's in English Literature in 2012 and a Master's in Teaching in 2015, both degrees from the University of Guam.

I taught Creative Writing, English ESL, English Honors, and ESL Math. Yup, MATH, a subject I failed three times in high school. After about three years in the classroom, I realized it wasn't where I wanted to be. In the summer of 2016, I moved to Denver, CO to pursue broader artistic and educational opportunities.

I'm writing this now on my cellphone debating if I should walk to Office Depot to get a working laptop. There's no comma in my bank account. My fridge is quite empty. I leave for a poetry competition tomorrow. I earned a spot on one of Denver's national poetry teams, Slam Nuba (WE CUT HEADS!), and I'll be traveling with them. I'm also preparing for my upcoming TEDxMileHigh talk. I hear giving a TEDx talk is on a few people's bucket lists. It wasn't on mine, but I'm glad I'll get to say it's something I did. I think an autobiography is supposed to focus solely on the past, never the future. I don't know how to not think about the future. Oh whale!

I think, in a nutshell, if an autobiography could be written in one sentence, I'd like mine to read: I go by Meta Sarmiento and a few people told me that my transformations have inspired transformations of their own. Yeah, that would be pretty dope!

www.reachmeta.com
@metasarmiento